JANE LONG
A Child's Pictorial History

JANE WILKINSON LONG
"Mother of Texas" / 1798–1880
— Courtesy Barker Texas History Center,
The University of Texas at Austin

By Elizabeth Dearing Morgan

Featuring photographs by

Nancy Dearing Johnson

EAKIN PRESS   ★   Austin, Texas

For our mother,
Jo Anne Holtzclaw Dearing

Library of Congress Cataloging-in-Publication Data

Morgan, Elizabeth Dearing.
  Jane Long : a child's pictorial history / by Elizabeth Dearing Morgan : featuring
photographs by Nancy Dearing Johnson. — 2nd ed.
    p.   cm.
  Includes bibliographical references.
  Summary: Text and photographs trace the life of the fearless pioneer who became
known as the Mother of Texas.
  ISBN 0-89015-861-4
  1. Long, Jane Herbert Wilkinson, 1798–1880 — Juvenile literature. 2. Pioneers
— Texas — Biography — Juvenile literature. 3. Women pioneers — Texas —
Biography — Juvenile literature. 4. Texas — Biography — Juvenile literature.
  [1. Long, Jane Herbert Wilkinson, 1798–1889. 2. Pioneers. 3. Texas — Biogra-
phy.] I. Johnson, Nancy Dearing, ill. II. Title.
  F389.L85M67   1992, 1996
  976.4'04'092--dc20
  [B]   92-17739
                                                                            CIP
                                                                             AC

Cover Illustration by Mark Mitchell

Contents

MRS. GEORGE W. BUSH
First Lady of Texas
— *Photo courtesy Andrea Ball, Executive Assistant*

Foreword

When Jane Long lived in Texas in the early 1800s, Texas was a wild frontier. It was a rugged, unforgiving place to live — especially for women. Jane blazed the dusty trails of the Lone Star State with hard work and determination. She endured many hardships, including the death of her husband and daughters. But Jane Long did not give up. She made a home and a name for herself in the Lone Star State.

She was one of many women who relentlessly crusaded for change and worked hard to make our state a better place. Jane Long was more than a pioneer. She was a farmer. She was a wife and mother. She became the head of her house when her husband died. She is known as the Mother of Texas.

Texas is unique and strong because of our blend of many cultures and traditions. It is also strong because of the many successful women in Texas history. Jane Long was a pioneer woman who set a great example. She was a woman who had true Texas spirit. The story of her life is an exciting adventure story.

Laura Bush

The Mannour of Truman's Place — Hughesville, Maryland. For a century, people have believed that Jane Long was born here. Although she was not, Jane most likely was familiar with this home. When Jane was young, this house and the one she was actually born in were connected by a county road. By the time Jane moved away from Maryland, no one was living in this house and it was in bad shape. Long after Jane left Maryland, the house was restored and had a second story added. Jane would probably not recognize the house as it looks today. She also would not recognize its name, since it has been called "the Mannour of Truman's Place" since the 1940s.

— *Courtesy of the owners, Mr. and Mrs. Douglas Fontein*

"The Daughter of Maryland"

Even while she was still alive, Jane Long was called "the Mother of Texas." She had incredible adventures as one of Texas' first settlers.

Jane has also been called "the Daughter of Maryland." She began her life there on July 23, 1798, on her family's plantation in Charles County. She started life with the name Jane Herbert Wilkinson.

Several books report that she was born in a house called "the Mannour of Truman's Place." It was built about 1760 and is located near the Patuxent River. But when that house was included on the National Register of Historic Places, a researcher found a mistake. He discovered that Jane's family never owned or lived in the house. The Wilkinson family owned a larger plantation to the east, and that is where Jane was born. By 1900, Jane's birthplace was known as "the Heights."

The actual birthplace of Jane Long. This house was built in the early 1700s on a piece of land later called "the Heights." In 1985 it was about to be torn down because its owners wanted a new home built on this land. Fortunately, someone bought the house and had it moved. It is in storage now, waiting to be put back together on a new piece of land.

— Photo by J. Richard Rivoire, architectural historian, La Plata, Maryland

2

Jane was the tenth child in her family. Her mother became very sick while giving birth to Jane. The doctor had already given up on baby Jane. He thought she was born dead, so he put her in a dresser drawer. Then he worked hard to save her mother's life.

Jane's mother did pull through. But then there were screams from the dresser drawer! Only then did they realize that baby Jane was alive after all. Jane would live most of her days like that. She would pull through when others gave up.

The Wilkinson family was well-to-do. They had a lot compared to other families of that time. When Jane was born they owned about thirty slaves.

Even rich people back then did not have things that most Americans have today. They did not have nice, clean indoor bathrooms that flush. Their bathrooms were outdoors. It would be very cold to get out of bed and go outside to use the restroom in the winter! So they would use a chamber pot and empty it outside in the morning.

Anne Herbert Dent Wilkinson, mother of "the Mother of Texas." This is a photograph of an oil painting. Where is the original painting today?

Jane's father, Captain William Mackall Wilkinson, had fought in the Revolutionary War. America had gained her independence from Britain in this war. The Revolutionary War ended in 1776. Unfortunately, Captain Wilkinson died before Jane was even one year old.

Jane's mother was Anne Herbert Dent Wilkinson. She got her unusual middle name from a famous ancestor named Lord Herbert. He had lived in England. Jane, her mother, her sister, and, later on, Jane's daughter all had Herbert for middle names.

Ann Herbert Wilkinson Chesley Miller — Jane's sister Ann was
married to Mr. Chesley in Maryland, but he died. Ann was a widow
when she moved to Mississippi with Jane and their mother. Then
she married Mr. Miller.

— Courtesy of her descendant, Mr. Jack Benoist

6

2

The Move to Mississippi

Since Jane's father was dead, her mother decided to move the family to Mississippi. She wanted to be closer to other relatives. Jane was thirteen when they moved. But the next year, her mother died. Jane was an orphan at age fourteen.

Jane did have her older sisters. They helped take the place of her mother. She moved in with one of them. Her sister was married and lived on a plantation in Washington, Mississippi. Washington was very close to the frontier town of Natchez.

Once again there has been a mistake about the house where Jane lived. Many books state that Jane lived with her sister, Barbara Wilkinson Calvit, at the Calvit plantation called Propinquity.

But the Calvits never owned Propinquity. They owned land nearby. Actually, another married sister of Jane's owned Propinquity. Her name was Ann Wilkinson Miller. The descendants of Ann Wilkinson Miller still live at Propinquity today.

General James Wilkinson, known to Spain as "Agent No. 13." To Jane Wilkinson Long he was known as "Uncle James."

— Courtesy National Portrait Gallery, Smithsonian Institution

Another relative of Jane's living in Mississippi was General James Wilkinson. He was famous because he apparently led a double life. He was an American general. He fought in the Revolutionary War like Jane's father. But he also worked for Spain.

He and another American named Aaron Burr tried to form their own country in Mexico. They were not successful. Eventually, they got into trouble by the United States for trying it. The United States did not want trouble with Mexico.

General Wilkinson was accused of being a traitor to the United States. The government did not like that he had worked for Spain and had tried to make problems with Mexico. But later he had his name cleared. He blamed things on Aaron Burr, so Burr was punished instead.

The mansion Propinquity in Washington, Mississippi, is as beautiful today as it was 200 years ago. This is where Jane spent her teen years.

— Photo by Nancy Dearing Johnson

Jane called General Wilkinson "Uncle James." But he was probably her second cousin, not her uncle. In either case, Jane's relative was a man who made history. Jane shared his taste for adventure.

The nation was changing. The War of 1812 was going on. The Americans were fighting the British again. The war ended with the Battle of New Orleans in 1815.

Natchez was not far up the Mississippi River from New Orleans. Many of the wounded American soldiers were taken to Natchez. They were cared for in private homes. One of those wounded soldiers stayed at Propinquity.

Jane was sixteen at the time. She went to school at a nearby academy. She had a slave maid named Kian. Kian was her friend.

One day a young doctor arrived at Propinquity to treat the wounded soldier. Kian rushed to stop Jane from going to school. Kian said that the "handsomest" man in the world was there. She said that Jane simply had to see him.

The staircase at Propinquity. Is this where Jane first laid eyes on her future husband?

— Photo by Nancy Dearing Johnson

It did not take much to talk Jane into missing school. She wanted to see for herself how handsome the doctor was.

Dr. James Long came down the stairs. Jane saw that he was not the "handsomest" man in the world. But he was an interesting man. He was a soldier as well as a doctor. In fact, he had fought at the Battle of New Orleans. General Andrew Jackson had praised him for being brave.

Jane and James introduced themselves. Then they decided to play a game of backgammon. They bet a pair of gloves on the outcome. James lost and brought Jane a pair of gloves the next day. Jane didn't want to accept the gloves from a bet. So James offered his hand in marriage along with the gloves. Soon they had fallen in love.

This portrait was said to have been painted while Jane Long was alive. Mr. Winston Farbar of Houston gave the oil painting to the George Foundation of Richmond, Texas. It is displayed at the Fort Bend Museum in Richmond.

— *Portrait owned by the George Foundation of Richmond, Texas; copy courtesy of UT Institute of Texan Cultures at San Antonio*

3

Mrs. Jane Long

Jane and James wanted to get married. But Jane's family did not want them to. They said she was too young. Sixteen does seem young today, but back then many girls were married at that age. People did not live as long as they can expect to today.

Maybe Jane's family was worried that James Long would not give Jane a very stable life. After all, he was a soldier. He was also the type of man who rushed into action. Sometimes he did things without thinking about what could happen.

Since Jane was an orphan, the law allowed her to choose her own guardian. When her family would not let her marry, she chose Dr. James Long as her guardian. They were married on May 14, 1815, at Propinquity. Her name became Mrs. Jane Long.

To please Jane and her family, James gave up being in the military. He went into business as a doctor in Port Gibson, Mississippi.

Twin bridges span the mighty Mississippi River at Vicksburg. The Longs probably lived very near this crossing because in this area was the village of Walnut Hills.

— *Photo by Nancy Dearing Johnson*

16

Very soon afterwards, James stopped practicing medicine. They moved to a plantation at Walnut Hills, Mississippi. Their plantation has sometimes been described as very grand. But this is highly unlikely. Walnut Hills was extremely rough territory at the time. It is now called Vicksburg. There are no traces of Jane's old home there. But this is where Jane's first child was born. When Jane was eighteen, she gave birth to a daughter. Jane named her Ann Herbert Long.

The year was 1816. When the Mississippi Territory took a count of all the people who lived there, Dr. James Long was on the list. He is shown as the head of a household of six. This means he and Jane may have had relatives living with them. The list, or census, also shows that the family owned twelve slaves.

In 1817 Dr. James Long still lived in Walnut Hills and was a merchant. He must have owned some type of store.

Jane Long holds the Texas Lone Star flag while Anson Jones, last
president of the Republic of Texas, looks over her shoulder. This is
part of the mural in the Hall of State at the Fairgrounds in Dallas.
— *Photo by Nancy Dearing Johnson*

A couple of years later, the Longs moved to Natchez, Mississippi. James became a merchant again.

The people of Natchez were upset when the United States gave away all claim to Texas. The Adams-Onís Treaty of 1819 gave Texas to Spain. Texas was just on the other side of Louisiana from Natchez. The Mississippians did not want the Spaniards to own Texas. They wanted America to own Texas.

A group of people in Natchez decided that they would go to Texas. They wanted to free it from Spanish rule. They elected James Long to be the leader of the group. From that point on, he was called General Long. Before little Ann turned three years old, her father went off to Texas to begin work.

Jane sent with him a flag. She and her sister, Ann Miller, had made the flag. They wanted it to fly over the new country of Texas. The flag was white with red stripes and fringe. It had a white star on a red background in the upper corner. This was the first Lone Star flag to fly over the Lone Star State.

In Jane Long's time, Natchez-Under-the-Hill was a very rough place. But today, Silver Street has nice restaurants and shops. They face the Mississippi River.

— *Photo by Nancy Dearing Johnson*

Jane wanted to go to Texas too. But she was going to have another baby. Traveling in the wild country would be too dangerous for her. It would not be good for a pregnant woman to ride horseback for hundreds of miles. And there were still Indian attacks on white settlers in Texas.

Jane stayed in Mississippi and had another daughter. Jane named her Rebecca.

Jane was very upset. She wanted to be with her husband. One day she took her two-week-old baby and two-and-a-half-year-old Ann down to the Mississippi River. The boat docks were in a very bad part of town. It was called Natchez-Under-the-Hill. They got on a boat to start for Texas.

The Old Stone Fort in Nacogdoches was built in the late 1700s to be used as a house. It was torn down in 1902. A replica of it was later built and is operated as a museum by Stephen F. Austin State University.

— Courtesy of the UT Institute of Texan Cultures, San Antonio

4

Jane Travels to Texas

The boat was leaky and uncomfortable. Jane and her daughters floated down the river to Alexandria, Louisiana. Jane's sister, Barbara Calvit, had moved there. Barbara would take care of the girls while Jane went to Texas to see her husband. She got to Texas by riding in a carriage the first part of the journey. Then she rode on muleback the rest of the way.

General Long was in Nacogdoches. He had captured the town so that he could say Texas was now an independent nation. He wanted it to be free from Spain. He made himself president of Texas. He and his men stayed in an old stone fort.

As soon as Jane got to Nacogdoches, though, James was getting ready to leave. He was going to Galveston. He wanted to ask the pirate Jean Lafitte for help in fighting the Spaniards. While he was gone, the Spanish army came to wipe out his fort at Nacogdoches. Jane escaped before the Spaniards got there. But all else was lost.

In this portion of the mural, James Long is shown riding his dapple gray horse. The mural is in the Hall of State at the Fairgrounds in Dallas.

— *Photo by Nancy Dearing Johnson*

The Longs went back to Louisiana. They were safe there from the Spaniards and Indians because they were on American soil. But there they received bad news. Their baby, Rebecca, had died. She died just days after Jane left her. They also learned that Indians had killed General Long's younger brother, David. David Long had been helping on the expedition.

Since he had lost control of Nacogdoches, General Long decided to set up his forces at Point Bolivar. Point Bolivar is a peninsula, or long strip of land, across from Galveston Island. Point Bolivar sticks out of the Texas coast into Galveston Bay in the Gulf of Mexico. In late 1820, Jane joined General Long. She brought her daughter, Ann, and her maid, Kian, with her. For almost a year, they lived happily at the mud fort.

Jean Lafitte, Pirate of the Gulf. There are lots of legends about Jean Lafitte. One says that when his girlfriend died, he buried her in his wine cellar.

*— Courtesy Center for American History
University of Texas at Austin*

Meeting Pirate Jean Lafitte

On Galveston Island, Jane could see Campeachy. This was the pirate Jean Lafitte's village. He had quite a following of men working for him. Jane was invited to eat dinner with Jean Lafitte on his ship. Her husband was not there at the time.

Jane thought that a pirate would be a very rough man. But she found that Jean Lafitte was very nice and polite. He didn't have much of a sense of humor, though.

He gave her a gift of a calling horn. It was a large steer horn that was used to send signals. The horn was carved to look like a fish. On its neck were the words "El Pirata," which means "The Pirate."

Some people wonder whether he really gave a gift that mentioned anything about "pirate" on it. Jean Lafitte did not call himself a pirate. He felt that he was helping America by raiding only Spanish ships.

This structure was built in the 1870s over the foundation and wine cellar of Jean Lafitte's Maison Rouge, or Red House. You can see it today in Galveston, Texas.

— *Photo by Nancy Dearing Johnson*

Jane was hoping to get Jean Lafitte to tell her his plans. She wanted him to say that he would help her husband's men. She wanted him to help them free Texas from Spain. But Lafitte had his own problems. The United States government did not want him on the Gulf Coast anymore. This was because sometimes his men attacked other ships besides Spanish ones.

The next day after Jane's dinner with him, Jean Lafitte left Galveston Island forever. He burned his big Red House to the ground. There is a legend that he left a fortune in treasure buried somewhere nearby.

The old Bolivar Lighthouse was built in 1872. Today it is privately owned. A granite marker there tells that this site was headquarters for Dr. James Long's expedition that tried — and failed — to free Texas, 1819–1821. It adds that Jane Long waited here for her husband. Because the marker doesn't say much about Jane's wait, author Ed Syers says he likes to think of the lighthouse as the monument to the Mother of Texas. He says that the lighthouse watches the sea, just as Jane did.

— Photo by Nancy Dearing Johnson

30

6

Alone!

One day word came that Mexico had declared its independence from Spain. Mexico considered Texas to be a part of Mexico.

James decided that he had better leave Point Bolivar to see what was actually going on. He told Jane to wait at the fort. He said that he would be back in three weeks. General Long left behind about fifty soldiers to guard the fort.

A month passed and General Long didn't return. Soldiers began to leave the fort. They took all the food and guns they could carry. Some doctors and their wives had been living at the fort too. Before they left, they begged Jane to go with them. But she would not go. "My husband left me here and I shall wait for him to return," Jane said each time someone asked her to leave.

Other people warned that if she stayed alone there she might starve. Also, she was going to have another baby soon. She would need a doctor. Besides these problems, there was the threat of Indians, Spaniards, and pirates. But Jane still would not leave.

Today you can ride the Bolivar Ferry from Galveston Island to Point Bolivar and feed the seagulls off the back of the boat. The free ferry ride is provided by the Texas Department of Highways and Public Transportation.

— Photo by Nancy Dearing Johnson

Finally, she was alone except for her six-year-old daughter, Ann, and her maid, Kian. Jane had learned many things at the academy back in Natchez. The academy was a place for wealthy young ladies to learn about things like manners and sewing. The academy did not teach young ladies how to hunt and fish — or to fight Indians! Jane was on her own. She would have to teach herself how to survive.

In December of 1821, a blizzard came. That was very unusual for Point Bolivar. Normally, winters are very mild on the coast. Jane and the girls moved into a tent, where it was a little warmer. But snow fell so hard that it ripped right through the tent.

Galveston Bay even froze over! Jane actually saw a big brown bear walk right across it. The bear did not even break the ice. Jane's dog, Galveston, chased the bear off. Galveston barked all the way.

This drawing accompanied an article on "Mrs. Jane Herbert Long" in an 1897 issue of *Texas Magazine*.

           — Courtesy of the Barker Texas History Center,
           The University of Texas at Austin

Jane certainly chose a bad year to be stranded on the Gulf Coast. It would not be cold enough to freeze the bay again for sixty-five years.

When Jane was ready to have her baby, no doctor was near to help her. Even her loyal maid Kian could not help. Kian had become very sick with a fever. She was so sick she didn't even know where she was. She couldn't get up at all.

Today most women go to the hospital to have a baby. The doctors and nurses take care of the mothers and babies. But Jane had to take care of herself, her sick friend, and her young daughter Ann, as well as the baby.

Jane gave birth on December 21, 1821. The wind was blowing snow onto her bed. She named the baby Mary James. Some people think that Jane named the baby after another Mary who gave birth in a manger long ago.

Many people say that Mary James Long was the first American child born in Texas. This is one of the reasons that Jane Long is called the "Mother of Texas."

This is a model of a bronze, life-size statue that will be placed on the Texas Capitol lawn by the Daughters of the Republic of Texas. It honors Texas pioneer women. Its face will be made to resemble Jane Long's. The artist is DRT member Linda Sioux Henley of San Antonio.

— *Photo courtesy DRT member Lel Hawkins*

7

Living On Oysters

There was no rest for Jane after the baby was born. The next morning she hunted food for her family. She and little Ann picked up fish. The fish had frozen close to the shore.

Kian soon got well and was able to help. One day they took their last fish hook and their only fishing line. They tried for a big fish. They got one, but Jane had tied the line to herself. She was being dragged toward the deep water so hard that she had to let go. She could see a big red fish swimming away.

This must have been very sad since they were left with no other way to fish. They had to live on oysters alone after that.

This scene shows what a Karankawa Indian camp may have looked like. You can see it at the Brazoria County Historical Museum in Angleton, Texas. Today historians believe that the Karankawas were not cannibals after all. Diorama created by Walter L. Vaughn of Lake Jackson, Texas.

— Photo by Nancy Dearing Johnson

38

Almost a month later, Jane was walking slowly down the beach. She noticed a string stuck in the sand. When she went to pick it up, she saw that it was the fishing line. It still had the hook and the large red fish on it!

Jane thought this was a miracle. After eating nothing but oysters, the red fish probably tasted pretty good.

Starving to death was not Jane's only problem. She and her family faced other dangers too. The Karankawa Indians lived on Galveston Island. Jane could see their campfires every night. Her husband and his men had fought them before. Her husband had told her that the Karankawas were cannibals. Cannibals are people who eat their enemies!

Stephen F. Austin said the Karankawa Indians "frequently feast on the bodies of their victims. There will be no way of subduing them except extermination." By 1858 they were considered extinct. This drawing appeared in the paper that Mrs. Mildred Pickle Mayhall wrote to earn her doctor of philosophy degree from the University of Texas in 1939. (Her report is located in the Benson Latin American Collection of The University of Texas at Austin.)

8

Karankawas!

Some of the Indians who lived in Texas were friendly. But the Karankawas were not. The Karankawas were very frightening because they were so large. Some people called them giants. Back then people were shorter than they are today. But most of the Karankawa men were over six feet tall. These fishermen were the tallest of all the Texas Indians.

The Karankawas were also scary looking because they stuck sticks through their lips and into their chests. They put tattoos on their bodies. In warm weather, the men often did not wear any clothes. In the winter, the men wore fur robes but no shoes.

They also smelled bad because they smeared their bodies with alligator grease and dirt. This kept the mosquitos away from them.

Kian often put on an old soldier's uniform. She wore it when she went to the beach to collect oysters. Jane and Kian hoped this would make the Indians think that the fort still had soldiers in it.

This picture of Jane Long was taken long after her Indian fighting days were over.

— Courtesy of the UT Institute of Texan Cultures, San Antonio

42

Jane taught Ann to play a game. They looked for footprints in the sand. Of course, Jane didn't tell the child that footprints were a warning. They meant unfriendly Indians were nearby!

One day the Karankawas came to the beach and got into canoes. Jane knew she was in trouble. She knew that if the Indians came to Point Bolivar, she had only one chance to survive. She had to trick the Indians. She had to make them think that the fort was still manned by soldiers. Then the Karankawas might leave the fort alone.

The soldiers had left a cannon at the fort. It was too heavy for them to carry away very easily. This was a lucky thing for Jane and her family. They needed it to protect themselves from the Karankawas.

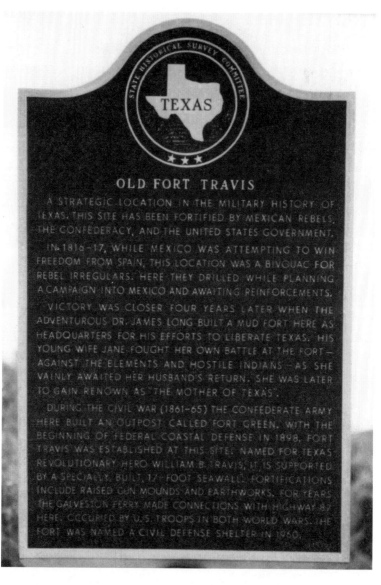

OLD FORT TRAVIS

A STRATEGIC LOCATION IN THE MILITARY HISTORY OF TEXAS, THIS SITE HAS BEEN FORTIFIED BY MEXICAN REBELS, THE CONFEDERACY, AND THE UNITED STATES GOVERNMENT.

IN 1816-17, WHILE MEXICO WAS ATTEMPTING TO WIN FREEDOM FROM SPAIN, THIS LOCATION WAS A BIVOUAC FOR REBEL IRREGULARS. HERE THEY DRILLED WHILE PLANNING A CAMPAIGN INTO MEXICO AND AWAITING REINFORCEMENTS.

VICTORY WAS CLOSER FOUR YEARS LATER WHEN THE ADVENTUROUS DR. JAMES LONG BUILT A MUD FORT HERE AS HEADQUARTERS FOR HIS EFFORTS TO LIBERATE TEXAS. HIS YOUNG WIFE JANE FOUGHT HER OWN BATTLE AT THE FORT — AGAINST THE ELEMENTS AND HOSTILE INDIANS — AS SHE VAINLY AWAITED HER HUSBAND'S RETURN. SHE WAS LATER TO GAIN RENOWN AS "THE MOTHER OF TEXAS".

DURING THE CIVIL WAR (1861-65) THE CONFEDERATE ARMY HERE BUILT AN OUTPOST CALLED FORT GREEN. WITH THE BEGINNING OF FEDERAL COASTAL DEFENSE IN 1898, FORT TRAVIS WAS ESTABLISHED AT THIS SITE. NAMED FOR TEXAS REVOLUTIONARY HERO WILLIAM B. TRAVIS, IT IS SUPPORTED BY A SPECIALLY BUILT 17-FOOT SEAWALL. FORTIFICATIONS INCLUDE RAISED GUN MOUNDS AND EARTHWORKS. FOR YEARS THE GALVESTON FERRY MADE CONNECTIONS WITH HIGHWAY 87 HERE. OCCUPIED BY U.S. TROOPS IN BOTH WORLD WARS. THE FORT WAS NAMED A CIVIL DEFENSE SHELTER IN 1960.

Mistake on the marker — The Texas Historical Commission is in the process of taking this marker down and putting up a new one. Researchers now believe that Jane Long was not near the site of Old Fort Travis, but on the other side of Port Bolivar.

— Photo by Nancy Dearing Johnson

44

Kian loaded the cannon and Jane set it off. She aimed at the giant Indians. Kian and Jane scared the Indians off.

Jane thought that to make the fort look like a real one, she needed to have a flag. But, of course, she didn't have a flag. She put her mind to work. What could she use instead?

What Jane ran up the flag pole wasn't a flag. But it surely helped keep the Karankawas away. It also kept Jane Long in stories passed down by many Texans for generations to come. What did Jane Long run up the flag pole? It was her red flannel petticoat!

This photo of a portrait of Jane was probably taken about fifty years ago. The painting was said to be made from an old daguerreotype (an early type of photograph). The authors could not find the actual oil painting. This portrait of Jane is very similar to the one on page 14. Some people think that, sometime after the above photo was taken, this portrait was painted over to make Jane look younger. They think that this portrait is actually the same as the one on page 14. If it is, that would explain why this portrait, where Jane is older looking, cannot be located!

— Courtesy Center for American History
University of Texas at Austin

9

Terrible News

Spring had come. Jane and her girls had been living at the fort a long time. James had been gone for six months.

One day a family passed by in a small boat. They offered to take Jane away from Point Bolivar. Finally, Jane agreed. They rowed up the bay. Jane and her girls ended up living in a hut. The place was called Rankins.

Jane learned that Mexico had won independence from Spain. Spain had owned Mexico and Texas, but not anymore. Jane was glad that Texas was free from Spain. But now Texas was owned by Mexico.

That summer Jane got a letter that contained bad news. She had hoped never to hear this news. The letter said her husband was dead.

General James Long had been captured and taken to Mexico City. One morning he was walking to a meeting. He was going to see a government official. But a guard ordered him to stop. James reached toward his pocket to show the guard his passport. The guard thought he was reaching for a gun and shot him. James Long died on the spot.

Benjamin Rush Milam promised to take care of Jane. But after he captured San Antonio during the Siege of Bexar, he was struck down by a sharpshooter.

— Courtesy Center for American History
University of Texas at Austin

Colonel Ben Milam had been with James earlier. On the night before he was killed, James told Colonel Milam that he had a bad feeling. James thought he would not live to see his family again. He asked Milam to take care of them.

Jane could not hope for her husband's return any longer. She was a widow at age twenty-four. She had two small daughters to support.

She decided to make the long trip to San Antonio. She wanted to see if she could get any money from the new government. Her husband had helped the new government in its fight against Spain.

There are no photos of Kian Long or her children. There are not even any photos of her grandchildren. But this is a photo of her great-granddaughters.

— *Courtesy of the UT Institute of Texan Cultures, San Antonio*

Searching for a Home

Jane, Kian, Ann, and the baby made the trip to San Antonio on horseback. Their friends, the Jones brothers, went with them. They went along to protect Jane and the girls. Three other men who worked for the Jones brothers came too. Between the nine people, they had three horses.

The group stopped at a lagoon for water near the Guadalupe River. There they met up with some Karankawa Indians. The Indians did not hurt them. There were also two Americans camping there. The men invited Jane's party to join them. But Jane insisted on crossing the river instead. It was a good choice. That night the Indians attacked and killed the other two men.

Jane and her party made it to San Antonio. There they had a place to stay. The people even gave them parties. But there was no money to be had.

Barbara Wilkinson Calvit, Jane Wilkinson Long's sister. This portrait was made around 1850. It belonged to Blakely Winston Pittman, a descendant of Jane Long. He gave it to the Fort Bend Museum in Richmond, Texas.

— Photo by Nancy Dearing Johnson

Eventually, Jane decided to take her family back to Louisiana. She wanted to see her sister, Barbara Calvit, who lived there. They rode with a pack train owned by a friend of Jane's.

One day the pack train stopped on the Brazos River. A widower who lived there gave watermelon to the entire group. His wife had just died. He proposed to Jane Long on the spot! She did not accept.

Finally, she reached her sister's in Louisiana. Soon her husband's friend, Ben Milam, showed up.

Colonel Milam gave Jane her husband's belongings. He gave her the blood-stained clothing James had been wearing when he was shot.

Milam told Jane that he thought that General Long's death was not an accident. The government had said it was an accident. But Milam and some others thought that James was killed on purpose. They believed his enemies in the government set it up.

Stephen F. Austin, the Father of Texas, was only a friend to the Mother of Texas.
— *Courtesy of the UT Institute of Texan Cultures, San Antonio*

Ben Milam worked to keep his promise to James. He took care of Jane and the girls. He saw that they made it safely to see Jane's other sister. She was Ann Miller, who lived in Mississippi. While Jane was there, something terrible happened.

The baby, Mary James, died. Mary had been one of the first American children born in Texas. She died in 1824. She was not even three years old.

Now Jane had lost her husband and two of her daughters. She had only her daughter Ann left. She and Ann and her maid, Kian, moved back to Texas the same year Mary James died. Jane's sister, Mrs. Calvit, and her family moved to Texas too.

They were all part of Stephen F. Austin's "Old Three Hundred." It was the first group of American settlers that the Mexican government let Austin bring into Texas.

Ann Herbert Long Winston Sullivan — The only child of Jane Long who lived to be an adult. Ann's first husband, Mr. Winston, died. She married again. Her second husband was Mr. Sullivan. The Sullivans moved to Bee County, Texas. Ann Sullivan's great-grand-daughter, Carrie Cochran Simons, gave this portrait to the Bee County Historical Society. They display it in the oldest house in Beeville, the McClanahan House, which is used as a museum.

— Photo by Nancy Dearing Johnson

11

Texas Settler

Jane became very good friends with Stephen F. Austin. This is only fitting, since he was later called the "Father of Texas." He was called that for settling so many Americans there.

Jane and her family lived in San Felipe de Austin. Then they moved to Fort Bend. They worked as farmers. They didn't have much money.

The years passed. Jane watched her daughter Ann grow up. When Ann was fifteen, Jane sent her back to Natchez, Mississippi, to go to school there.

The next year Ann was married. She married at age sixteen, just like her mother. She became Mrs. Ann Long Winston. Ann and her husband moved to Texas. They stayed with Jane.

In 1832, Jane opened a boarding house in Brazoria. The boarding house was very popular with many men. Some of them became famous in Texas history.

SITE OF JANE LONG'S TAVERN

JANE HERBERT WILKINSON (1798-1880) WAS BORN IN MARYLAND AND MOVED TO NATCHEZ, MISSISSIPPI, IN 1812. THERE IN 1815 SHE MARRIED PHYSICIAN AND SOLDIER JAMES LONG (c.1793-1822). JANE WAS GRANTED LAND IN AUSTIN'S COLONY IN 1827, AND OPENED A BOARDING HOUSE ON THIS SITE IN 1832. THE BUSY PORT AND TAVERN BECAME A POPULAR CENTER OF ANGLO POLITICAL ACTIVITY. HERE JANE HOSTED A BENEFIT FOR STEPHEN F. AUSTIN IN 1835, UPON HIS RELEASE FROM MEXICAN PRISON, AND A BALL IN OCTOBER, 1836, ATTENDED BY PRESIDENT SAM HOUSTON AND THE ADJOURNED CONGRESS. SHE MOVED TO RICHMOND IN 1837 TO OPERATE A POPULAR HOTEL THERE.

TEXAS SESQUICENTENNIAL 1836-1986

This marker can be seen at the corner of Main and Market streets in Brazoria, Texas. Just across the street is the Brazos River. Brazoria is known as the "Cradle of Texas Liberty."

— *Photo by Nancy Dearing Johnson*

There are not very many boarding houses around anymore. Boarding houses are different from hotels because a boarding house is actually someone's home. The owner lives there and has guests pay to rent a bedroom. The owner cooks the meals and the guests eat in the dining room. The guests are like part of one big family. Jane got to know the Texan leaders well since they stayed at her boarding house.

Many of the Texan settlers were unhappy. They did not like the way they were treated by the Mexican government. They sent Stephen F. Austin down to Mexico City. He was going to speak with the men in charge. But they did not help him or even listen to him. Instead they put him in jail for a year and a half.

When they let Austin go, he went back to Texas. He spoke to a huge crowd at Jane Long's boarding house. There were probably one thousand people at Jane's. Austin made a strong speech. He called for Texans to band together. He said Texans should declare their independence from Mexico.

The year was 1835. Within a couple of months, the Texas Revolution would begin.

The Brazos River. This is how it looks from the site of Jane Long's Tavern in Brazoria, Texas. People came to her boarding house by way of the river as well as the road.

— Photo by Nancy Dearing Johnson

60

12

Texans at the Tavern

Jane's inn had a brick outhouse behind it. An outhouse is an outdoor restroom. Jane's outhouse held a secret. The first gun powder to be used for the Texas Revolution was stored there!

The Texans had to hide the gun powder for the Revolution. That way the Mexicans would not know that the Texans were planning to fight.

The Mexican government had already sent a man to Texas. His name was Colonel Juan Almonte. He was supposed to see what was going on in Texas.

Colonel Almonte stayed at Jane Long's. Everyone was nice to him. They told him that the Texans were not thinking of war.

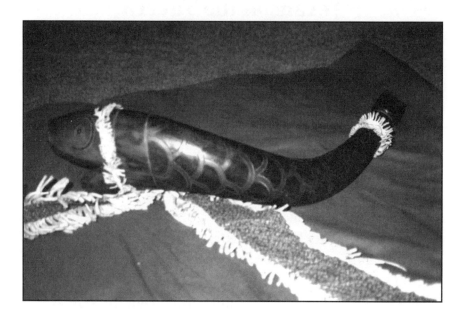

This is the calling horn that Jean Lafitte gave to Jane Long, and Jane Long gave to Sam Houston, and Sam Houston gave to Robert Hall. It is now owned by Robert Hall's descendant, Steve Strobel, of Boulder, Colorado. When a person blows into the tail, sound comes out the mouth.

— Photo courtesy Jan Strobel

But indeed the Texans did fight. Jane lost her good friend Ben Milam. He was killed after he captured the town in the Siege of Bexar.

Another famous Texan had stayed at Jane Long's boarding house. He was William Barret Travis. Travis was a young attorney. He became a colonel in the Texas army. He was the commander of the Alamo. Travis wrote a letter from the Alamo to the people of Texas. He said that he would never surrender or retreat. That letter made him famous. He signed the letter "VICTORY OR DEATH." Unfortunately for him and Texas, he got the latter, death.

Every man at the Alamo died a hero's death. They were remembered by their fellow Texans. After that, the other Texans rushed into battle crying, "Remember the Alamo!"

This famous painting shows Mexican General Santa Anna (1) sur-
rendering to Texan General Sam Houston (2). General Houston is
lying down because his leg was hurt in the battle. Standing by is
Colonel Juan Almonte (3). He had stayed at Jane Long's boarding
house. In the background is Jane's friend Mirabeau B. Lamar (4).
The original of this painting hangs in the state capitol at Austin.
— *Courtesy of the UT Institute of Texan Cultures, San Antonio*

General Sam Houston was another of Jane's guests at her boarding house. He went off to battle too. It is said that Jane Long gave General Houston her calling horn before he left. This was the horn that Jean Lafitte had given her. Maybe the calling horn did give General Houston good luck. He tasted victory at the Battle of San Jacinto. He crushed the Mexican General Santa Anna's forces. This battle won independence for Texas.

General Houston's win at the Battle of San Jacinto was in 1836. After that, Texas was its own country. No other government gave its citizens orders. Jane was very happy. That is what her husband James had wanted. That is what he wanted to do when he came to Texas many years before.

Sam Houston visited Jane Long's boarding house often. He was later elected president of the Republic of Texas. There was gossip going around that Jane and Sam Houston were sweethearts.

Mirabeau B. Lamar served as the president of the Republic of Texas. He once proposed to "bonnie Jane." The original of this daguerrotype can be seen at the San Jacinto Museum of History located at the San Jacinto Monument near Houston.

— Courtesy San Jacinto Museum of History

The vice-president of the Republic of Texas was Mirabeau B. Lamar. Lamar was very fond of Jane. He spent a great deal of time with her. Jane told him the story of her husband's life. He wrote it all down. This story is written in a collection called the *Lamar Papers*. The information helped people learn about Jane's life too.

Jane and Mirabeau B. Lamar were very close. Eventually, Mirabeau asked Jane to marry him. Lamar even wrote a poem dedicated to "bonnie Jane." The poem described his love for her. But Jane would not marry him. She still had a deep feeling for her dead husband. After about ten years, Lamar changed the name in his poem. He called it "bonnie Ann." Jane never did marry again.

Jane Long Boarding House

The historical marker on this site says, "During the period Texas was a colony and a republic, Jane Long operated two well-known boarding houses. She started the first in Brazoria in 1832. Her guests included William B. Travis, Sam Houston, and Mirabeau B. Lamar. In 1837 Jane moved to Richmond and on this site opened another boarding house which became a center for social and political activities as well as lodging for prominent Texans and European visitors. Jane ran this hotel until her plantation near town became prosperous in 1840s." After Jane Long's death, the house was torn down. Today you can see the marker in an empty lot at 101 North Fourth Street near downtown Richmond, Texas.

— Courtesy Fort Bend Museum, Richmond, Texas

13

War Between the States

In 1837, Jane moved her boarding house from Brazoria to Richmond. Her boarding house served as campaign headquarters for Mirabeau B. Lamar. He ran for president of the Republic of Texas and won. Her inn was also the home away from home for another Texas president. His name was David G. Burnet.

But soon she closed the boarding house down altogether. Her plantation began making more money. It began to support her comfortably.

Texas became one of the United States in 1845. By that time Jane's plantation had become one of the most valuable in the entire state of Texas.

Things seemed to be quiet in Texas. Jane was entering her later years. But then another crisis hit her state.

Jane Long when she was about sixty. By this time Jane was a wealthy plantation owner. This ambrotype (an early type of photograph) was taken around 1858.

— *Courtesy Center for American History*
University of Texas at Austin

Jane had already lived through the War of 1812. She had lived through the Mexican and Texas revolutions. Now she was sixty-three years old. And she was about to see the coming of the Civil War, also known as War Between the States.

This war was fought between the northern and southern states of the United States of America. The battles started in 1861. The North and the South had different ways of life. The South felt that they were not being represented in Congress. The southern states wanted to control their own affairs.

Finally, the southern states decided that they no longer wanted to be part of the United States of America. They formed themselves into the Confederate States of America. They wanted to have a revolution to free themselves from the United States. The northern states felt that it was illegal for the southern states to leave the U.S. The northern states fought to keep the southern states in the Union. The issue was over slavery practiced in the South.

Mary Ann Sullivan Miles — Jane Long's granddaughter, Mary Ann
Sullivan, was the daughter of Ann Long and her second husband,
James Sullivan. Mary Ann married Mr. Miles. This portrait hangs
in the McClanahan House in Beeville, Texas.

— Photo by Nancy Dearing Johnson

Jane was very glad that Texas joined the Confederacy. She worked hard to send clothing and other things to the southern soldiers. She also refused to wear any clothing that was made outside the South.

By this time Jane had two grandchildren, James and Mary. They were her daughter Ann's children. Jane watched her grandson, James Winston, march off to fight for the Confederate army.

By 1865, the war was over. More Americans were lost in that war than in any other before or since. Land and buildings were burned or destroyed too.

The South had lost the war. And people from the South had lost their entire way of life. Things were not better for the Confederates after the war. Things were much worse for them.

This photo was taken around the time of the War Between the States. Before this book, this photo had never been published or displayed. It is owned by Jane's sister's descendant, Jack Benoist of Washington, Mississippi.

— *Courtesy Jack Benoist, Washington, Mississippi*

But Texas was not as hard hit as the other southern states. Most of the battles had taken place farther east. Texas was still on the edge of the frontier.

When the war ended, Texas and all the other Confederate states became part of the United States again. They have remained so until this day.

Jane's plantation was not affected very much. The end of the war did signal the end of slavery, though. This meant Kian was no longer bound to Jane. But Kian continued to work for Jane anyway. Kian's daughter, Clarisa, also worked for Jane. And Kian's granddaughter, also named Kian, worked for Jane too.

The Civil War was over, and Jane Long was still going strong at about age seventy-two. This ambrotype was taken around 1870.

— *Courtesy Center for American History*
University of Texas at Austin

14

Last Days in Richmond

The years passed. Jane sat in her rocking chair on her front porch. She smoked a tobacco pipe. She grew the tobacco on her plantation. She lived to be an old woman in Richmond.

Her lifelong friend, Kian, and her daughter, Ann, both died before Jane did. But Jane had the company of her two grandchildren, James and Mary. James and Mary gave her seven great-grandchildren.

Kian's daughter and granddaughter also gave Jane comfort and friendship to the end. It was Kian's granddaughter, the younger Kian, who took Jane on her last carriage ride. They rode through the town of Richmond. Even as Jane was coming to the end of her life, she had a sense of humor. She also had a sense of independence.

On her ride, she went to visit her doctor first. She told him not to help her down from the carriage. Jane joked that he might "let her fall." Then she stopped to see her granddaughter Mary and her friend Clarisa. Finally, she stopped to eat at an ice cream parlor.

Morton Cemetery's historical marker says, "Burial place of illus-
trious pioneers, including . . . one of state's first women settlers,
Jane Long (1798–1880), known as 'the Mother of Texas'." Even her
tombstone bears the sobriquet, or nickname, "Mother of Texas."
— *Photo by Nancy Dearing Johnson*

Jane held on to her life throughout the next month. She celebrated Christmas with her family. Finally, she died on December 30, 1880. She was eighty-two years old.

Jane had loved Texas very much. Her husband had given his life for Texas. Jane herself had worked to free Texas from Spain. Then she had worked to free Texas from Mexico. She was proud to be a part of Texas when it was a country all its own. Jane was there when Texas became a part of the United States. She was glad when Texas left to become a part of the Confederate States. And she saw the final change that brought Texas back into the United States of America again.

Jane Herbert Wilkinson Long is buried in the cemetery at Richmond, Texas. She rests there along with other Texas heroes, such as her friend, Mirabeau B. Lamar.

Jane Long will always be remembered as the fearless pioneer of American women in Texas.

Afterword

Jane Long gave birth to one of the first American children born in Texas. But some historians say Jane's child was not *the* first. Hers may have been the second American child born in Texas. Even so, Jane would still deserve her nickname, "Mother of Texas." She deserves the nickname because she spent her entire life fighting for Texas' freedom.

Although Jane is gone, there are several monuments in Texas that pay tribute to her. Photographs of these monuments follow.

Jane Long Elementary School (Lamar Consolidated ISD) was built on the site of the old Richmond High School in 1948. It houses 3rd through 5th grades.

— *Courtesy of Pat Dudley, principal*

Jane Long Primary on Ninth Street in Richmond houses K–2nd graders.

The Pre-K classroom for Jane Long Elementary used to be the old Richmond High School Home Economics Building.

— Photos by Nancy Dearing Johnson

81

Also in Richmond is the Jane Long Annex, owned by Fort Bend County.

Jane Long League Drive is a street in the Pecan Grove Plantation area of Richmond.

— *Photos by Nancy Dearing Johnson*

Jane Long Elementary School (Brazosport ISD) in Freeport, Texas, houses K–5th. It was called West Freeport Elementary when it opened in 1952. In the early 1960s, its name was changed to Jane Long Elementary School.

— Courtesy Robin Bowlin

Jane Long Elementary School (Midland ISD) in Midland, Texas, was built in 1955 or 1956. It serves as the neighborhood school for K–3rd graders, and it is the "cluster" school for 4th graders. That means it has fifteen 4th-grade classes!

— Courtesy Provine Studios of Alexandria, Louisiana

When Jane Long won out over Albert Sidney Johnston as the name for the new West Bellaire Area Junior High School in 1957, it became one of the first secondary schools in Houston, Texas, to be named for a woman. The school was named "in honor of an early pioneer in Texas history who is often referred to as the Mother of Texas." Today it is called Jane Long Middle School (Houston ISD).

—Photo by Nancy Dearing Johnson

Jane Long Elementary School (Abilene ISD) in Abilene, Texas, was named to honor the "Mother of Texas" for her pioneering spirit. It was built in 1959 and houses K-5th graders.

— Courtesy of Pat Dudley, principal

Jane W. Long Elementary School (Harlingen Consolidated ISD) in Harlingen, Texas, was built in 1985. Harlingen schools are named for Texas heroes, and Jane W. Long was chosen because she was the "Mother of Texas." The school has Pre-K through 6th grades and is one of the largest elementary schools in its district.

— *Courtesy Sonia Brown, Harlingen CISD*

Jane Long Junior High School (Bryan ISD) in Bryan, Texas, is the newest school to be named after the "Mother of Texas." It was built in 1989. Since then, it has become Jane Long Middle School and has 6th–8th graders.

— *Courtesy of Rebecca Larkin, assistant principal*

Daughters of the American Revolution

The National Society of the Daughters of the American Revolution (DAR) is a group of women whose ancestors worked for the nation's independence. The goal of members is to promote the memory of the spirit of these men and women. Also, they promote education and love of our country.

Since Jane Wilkinson Long's father, Capt. William Mackall Wilkinson, served in the Revolutionary War, she was a true Daughter of the American Revolution. In Pasadena, Texas, the Jane Long chapter of the DAR was formed in 1973 and was named to honor the Mother of Texas. Today it has over 100 members. There is also a Children of the American Revolution chapter. The children's chapter, called the Mary James Long Society, was named after Jane's baby who was born in Texas.

Daughters of the Republic of Texas

The Daughters of the Republic of Texas (DRT) are women whose ancestors were loyal Texas citizens before Texas became a state in 1846. Their goal is to promote the memory of Texas pioneer families and soldiers of the Republic of Texas.

The DRT has a chapter in Kingsville, Texas, that is named after Jane Long. When the chapter was being formed in 1976, members chose to name it for Jane Long because they wanted to honor a female pioneer.

Do You Know?

There are still some mysteries about Jane Long.

For example, in 1969, Jane Long's branding iron was listed as a "museum piece in the state capitol." Her cattlebrand was J-L (to stand for JHL, or Jane Herbert Long). Believed to have been the first registered in Texas, the cattlebrand is no longer in the state capitol. But where is it?

And what about Jane Long's birthplace? Will the 270-year-old house ever find a piece of land where it can be put back together again to serve as a tribute to pioneer history?

A study guide to *Jane Long: A Child's Pictorial History* is available. Included is an adult and children's bibliography, glossary, recipes, puzzles, timeline, drawing and coloring pages, and study questions. If you would like information about the study guide, please write to Eakin Press, P.O. Drawer 90159, Austin, Texas 78709-0159.

If you have any comments or questions about Jane Long, please write to the authors, Elizabeth Dearing Morgan or Nancy Dearing Johnson, in care of Eakin Press.

Celebrating Jane Long in March

March is a great month to celebrate the life of Jane Long, Mother of Texas. This is because March is Women's History Month throughout the United States, and also because March contains several Texas Honor Days.

March is Women's History Month

March 2nd is Texas Independence and Flag Day

March 6th is Alamo Heroes Day

March 27th was the Massacre at Goliad

Recipes

These recipes or "receipts" were taken from *Jane Long's Brazoria Inn: An Early Texas Cookbook* by Neila Skinner Petrick and Lorraine Savarese Dittmer. They are actually the type of recipes that were used in Jane Long's times.

*   *   *

Sugared Almonds

When Jane and her family visited San Antonio, one of her hosts was Texas patriot Don Seguin. Sugared Almonds is a treat that he may have served his guests. This candy is like Almond Brittle.

2 cups whole almonds, blanched
1 cup loaf sugar (regular sugar will do)

4 tablespoons fresh butter
1 teaspoonful essence of vanilla

(**Note:** To blanch the almonds, put them in a pan of boiling water for a short time. Then you'll be able to slip the skins right off.)

Heat almonds in heavy iron skillet with sugar and fresh butter. Stir the ingredients constantly until almonds are toasted and the sugar turns a golden color. Depending on the heat of the fire, this requires from 12 to 17 minutes. Then you add your flavoring, essence of vanilla or maybe some other if you have it. Spread the concoction out on a clean board to cool. You might sprinkle on a little salt to bring out the flavor. This will make nearly a pound.

*   *   *

Texas Pecan Fudge

Perhaps Texas Pecan Fudge was enjoyed as dessert for Jane Long's Christmas Day Dinner.

3 cups sugar
Heaping tablespoonful of grated cocoa
1 cup milk

1 tablespoon sweet butter
Add essence of vanilla
1/2 cup pecans

Combine sugar, cocoa, milk and butter. Cook over a low fire stirring constantly. When the candy begins to thicken, put a little bit into the cold water. If it forms a soft ball remove the candy from the fire. Add the essence of vanilla. Then beat the candy very hard, until creamy but not dry. Fold in your pecans and swiftly turn out into a buttered pan. When the candy sets, cut it into squares.

* * *

Pecan Pralines

Pecan pralines may have been served at the Old 300's first Thanksgiving at San Felipe de Austin. Jane first tasted them when she went with her husband Dr. James Long to New Orleans in 1821.

Pralines began as a French confection named for Marshall Cesar du Plessis-Praslin. His cook invented them. In other places they are not always made with pecans, but they are in Texas because the nut is so plentiful.

1 pound dark brown sugar	**Speck of salt**
¾ cup rich cream	**1 tablespoon butter**
½ pound of pecan halves	
(about 2 teacupfuls)	

Take a heavy pan and mix together all ingredients save for the pecans. Cook over a low fire until the sugar dissolves, stirring faithfully. Now you add your pecans and add another stick of wood to the fire to get it hotter. Cook and stir until a soft ball forms in a teacup of water. Remove from fire immediately and let cool. Once your mixture begins to thicken, drop by spoonfuls onto a greased surface. If the candy begins to stick to the spoon too much add some boiling water from your tea kettle. Cool and serve.

The parlor at Propinquity.

— Photo by Nancy Dearing Johnson

The Texas Historical Commission erected this marker at the site of Jane Long's Boarding House in 1975.

— *Photo by Nancy Dearing Johnson*

The Long-Smith Cottage was built on Jane's property in the 1840s.
It was moved to the Fort Bend Museum (Richmond, Texas) in 1987.
— *Photo by Nancy Dearing Johnson*

Words to Know

backgammon: a board game like checkers.

cannibal: a person who eats human flesh.

census: an official count of the people of a country.

descendants: offspring, such as children, grandchildren, etc.

frontier: the last edge of settled country.

generations: people born in the same period of time, about twenty to thirty years apart.

government: persons ruling a country.

guardian: person who takes care of someone who is young.

independence: freedom.

lagoon: a pond connected with a larger body of water.

mannour: (more commonly spelled manor) a large estate.

mansion: a manor house.

merchant: a storekeeper.

National Register of Historic Places: list of places that are important because of their style or their history.

official: a person who is in charge of some public duty.

pack train: a caravan of horses and mules.

passport: a paper giving a citizen permission to travel in a foreign country.

peninsula: a piece of land extending far out into the water.

plantation: a large farm.

stable: secure; doesn't change much.

traitor: a person who betrays his country.

well-to-do: having enough money to live well.

Selected Bibliography

Bell, Alexander. *The Daughter of Maryland Was the Mother of Texas*. Washington, DC: The Law Reporter Printing Company, 1935.

Benoist, John "Jack." Interviews with the descendant of Ann Herbert Wilkinson Chesley Miller, who is the current owner of Propinquity mansion. Washington, Mississippi, 1989, 1991.

Brindley, Anne. "Jane Long." *Southwestern Historical Quarterly,* Volume LVI. Austin: Texas State Historical Association, October 1952.

Briscoe, Mary Jane, and Adele Briscoe Looscan. "Sketch of the Life of Mrs. Jane Long." 1882. Barker Texas History Center, The University of Texas at Austin.

Crawford, Ann Fears. *Jane Long — Frontier Woman*. Austin: W. S. Benson and Company, 1990.

Farbar, Winston. Interview with Jane Long's great-great-great-grandson. Houston, 1991.

Gonzalez, Catherine. *Jane Long, the Mother of Texas*. Burnet: Eakin Press, 1982.

Harrison, Nan Hillary. "Jane Long, the Mother of Texas: The Most Courageous and Incomparable Woman Pioneer in the Annals of History." After 1935. Barker Texas History Center, The University of Texas at Austin.

Houston Telegraph, May 27, 1871.

Lamar, Mirabeau Buonaparte. "Jane Long" from *Life of James Long*. Houston: Mirabeau Buonaparte Lamar, 1838.

Moore, Effie. *Alone by the Sea*. San Antonio: The Naylor Company, 1951.

Petrick, Neila Skinner. *Jane Long of Texas*. Austin: Prime Time Press, 1995.

Petrick, Neila Skinner and Lorraine Savarese Dittmer. *Jane Long's Brazoria Inn: An Early Texas Cookbook*. Dallas: Coldwater Press, 1992.

Seale, Jan Epton. *The Slave Girl Who Helped Start Texas — Kian Long*. McAllen, Texas: The Knowing Press, 1986.

Turner, Martha. *The Life and Times of Jane Long*. Waco: The Texian Press, 1969.

Acknowledgments

Thank you to our sons, Clint Morgan, Jason Johnson, and Justin Johnson, who endured numerous trips to strange places where Jane Long had been.

Thanks to their fathers, Tom Morgan and Louis Johnson, and their grandparents, Jo Anne and Olin Dearing, for helping take care of them when we were traveling child-free.

Thank you to publisher Ed Eakin and editor Melissa Roberts for their continuing commitment to Texas history.

Thanks to Steve and Jan Strobel for sharing photos of the fish-shaped calling horn.

Index

About the Author and Photographer

Elizabeth Dearing Morgan and her sister, **Nancy Dearing Johnson,** have traveled throughout Texas, Louisiana, and Mississippi doing original research and collecting never-before published photos to document the life of Jane Wilkinson Long. They are descended from a Miss Wilkinson who lived in Jane's home state of Maryland in the 1700s.

Their other books include *President Mirabeau B. Lamar: Father of Texas Education,* a photobiography of the Texas revolutionary hero who was Jane Long's close friend. Their newest release is *Texas Christmas: As Celebrated Under Six Flags,* which gives the history behind our Lone Star holiday traditions.

Morgan is an eighth-generation Texan and member of the Daughters of the Republic of Texas; tenth-generation Southerner and member of the United Daughters of the Confederacy; and eleventh-generation American and member of the Daughters of the American Revolution. All four of her grandparents were born in Texas, and all eight of her great-grandparents lived and died in Texas.

Elizabeth is a Texas secondary schoolteacher certified in social studies, reading, English, business, and home economics.

For autographings or author visits, contact the publisher at (512) 288-1771.

Elizabeth Morgan
— Photo by John Neely

Nancy Johnson
— Photo by Elizabeth Morgan